Cat and Dog

Written and illustrated by
Shoo Rayner
Collins

4

14

Ideas for reading

Written by Alison Tyldesley, MA PGCE
Education, Childhood and Inclusion Lecturer

Learning objectives: Using terms about books and print; tracking story in the right order; using story language to retell stories; retelling narratives in the correct sequence; asking and answering questions about living things.

Curriculum links: Knowledge and Understanding of the World: Find out about some features of living things

Getting started

- Pass a book to each child with the spine pointing forward. Ask which way up it goes. Talk about the front cover, author, illustrator and title.
- Ask the children to predict what the book is about from the front cover. Do the cat and dog look friendly? Why not?
- Look at the first few pages and ask how the book tells the story. Is anything missing or different from other books? (It is a book without words.)

Reading and responding

- Walk through the book up to p13, and model how to tell the story in your own words. Use story language. Stop at p9 and ask children to predict what happens.
- Ask the children if their prediction was right. Discuss the pictures on pp10–11. Ask why they think the dog helped the cat.
- Ask the children to use their finger to track the left-to-right sequence of the dog chasing the cat.
- When you've finished the story, look at pp14–15. What did the people think when they saw the dog and cat coming towards them again?
- Ask the children to tell the story to a partner. Encourage the children to use story language.